BOOK BENCHERS PUBLICATION

PRESENTS

BEHIND YOUR SHADOW

COMPILED BY

SANJAY NAIK

ANAMIKA

AELAY PUBLICATION

A dream come true for every writers out there. We spot every possible problem for the writers, help in rectifying them and guide them towards the best outcome. We make sure to understand your needs, dreams and expectations, and nourish them with our services and stop not until we fulfill your dreams. The writers have a right and freedom to choose what they want here. They have us to guide them through the hardest path until the end. Believe in us.

Aelay Publication - by a writer for the writers.

BOOK BENCHERS

Book Benchers is the affiliate of Aelay publication. Both the publication is handled by Irudaya Astro.
Aelay plays the role of publishing solo books. And Book Benchers is epically for publishing anthologies.

Book Benchers have 2 different teams.
1. Tamil

2. English/Hindi

Never mind what our main motive is to help all the budding writers, who are seeking for their dream of publishing their own book to come true.

We are there to help out everyone.
In guiding for starting up with your carrier in compiling until finishing up your full book.

ISBN-978-93-91423-71-1

Pages- 120

ACKNOWLEDGMENT

Acknowledgement is essential to boost up passion, making person more valid and precious, giving the team a great progress that makes worth.

We would like to use this opportunity to thank each and every one who all the people involved in this book and, more specifically, to all the co - authors .Without your support, this book would not have become a reality.

We would like to thank each one of the authors for their contributions. Our sincere gratitude to all who contributed their time and expertise to this book.

We wish to acknowledge the valuable contributions of the Publication regarding the improvement of quality, coherence, and content. Last but not least, we would like to extend our gratitude to parents and friends who have been a huge support through the book.

DISCLAIMER

This is a work of fiction. We strictly prohibited the function of plagiarism. Our team has work great enough to restrict the act of plagiarism. We never approach and support the plagiarism in any case. Still, If any writeup is detected, we won't responsible, the particular author is only responsible for the act. We insist and guide each and every Co- author to submit the original content.

<u>FOUNDER</u>

IRUDAGA ASTRO

Irudaga Astro, From Tirunelveli, Founder of
Aelay and BB (Book Benchers)
He had completed his BE.
He has written 3 Tamil poetry book's which hits
the top list on social media!
His main aim is to allow the writers to publish
their words as their book rather than just Posting
them on Insta.

LINK AND POSTER MAKER

CATHERINE ASMI T

Catherine Asmi T, From Tirunelveli
She has completed her M.com
Her passion is Drawing and Designing.

<u>TEAM HEAD</u>

She is a passionate writer from Chennai. Writing makes her pressure go away. She had played the role of co-author for more than 100+ Antho's.
She would like to thank her parents and her Loveable Brother for supporting her rather than stopping her from what she wanted to do! For being the main reason for achieving her dreams. As well as for standing beside her in all the ups and downs. Whenever she feels like she needs to get out of her stressful timing or feels like she needs peacefulness, she starts to paint, she would never mind sitting in the same place for so many hours when it comes to her painting. She believes that anyone could hurt her, But never her books could!!

Catch her in Insta and FB
Insta: @theinnocentheart
FB: KA. PARINASRI

INDEX - COMPILERS

SANJAY NAIK

ANAMIKA

CO – AUTHORS

(HINDI)

1.   Antara Choudhury
2.   Shivam Maurya
3.   Har Deepansh Bahadur Sinha
4.   Sonali Meher
5.   Kalamkaar
6.   Ankur Mishra
7.   Prakash Turiya (Raghuwanshi)
8.   Prakhar Raghuwanshi
9.   Priyanshu Kumar Pandey
10.   Shivang Sharma
11.   Poetry Khakholia
12.   Ankita Nahar
13.   Ravishanker Nishad (Arvi)
14.   Bhawna Mehta
15.   Anjali Samundre
16.   Yogesh Gurjar Chinu
17.   Kajal Bhargav
18.   Aayushi Khedia

(ENGLISH)

19.   Lipsa Dabhi
20.   Mohammed Niyaz
21.   Harshita Verma
22.   Priya Singh
23.   Dhritishree Rani Baruah
24.   Shaswat Sourav Sahoo (Shassy)
25.   Prachi Gupta

26.   Sakshi jarandikar
27.   S.Suganthi
28.   Madhumitha / madhu
29.   Sonal Prajapati
30.   Akkshaya prasanna
31.   Ankita Mishra
32.   Ananya P Mishra
33.   Dakshita jaiswal
34.   Dharshini. M
35.   Srija Sadhukhan
36.   Mansi Solanki
37.   Anusha Sathia
38.   Naveen Bhardwaj
39.   Rozy Paul
40.   Tahreem Afzal
41.   Surangama
42.   Deesha Soni
43.   Sonali Gouda
44.   Sheethal. G
45.   Unnati Sawant
46.   Varshitha Madhu
47.   N. Krishnaveni
48.   Habiba Naz
49.   Anupama Sahu
50.   Neeraj.J

COMPILER

SANJAY NAIK

Sanjay Naik is from Kharagpur State of West Bengal. He is an Economics graduate (Hons), a writer from the heart and passionate about singing. Through the platform of anthology, he wants to spread love & positivity among his readers and wants to heal his readers' hearts with his magical words. Sanjay is at utmost peace when he pens his emotions. He believes that the power of his words, will heal the wounds of many readers. Till now participated in 200+ Anthologies as a CO-AUTHOR. He is Compiler of anthology "SELF HAPPINESS" , "SCREAM" & " SARANG". And now Compiled more than 50 + Anthologies. Instagram:- @the_poetry_wo

ENLIGHTENMENT IN YOUR WORDS

I have a deep connection with words

Which thrives in my mind inside only

The mind is eager to know

The meaning of every word

This is my means of fulfilment

It has explained to me the definition of life

Has never even made me feel alone whenever the
mind feels heavy

Take a pen and write two words

It seems like I am blessed

To have enlightenment

It makes me happy to be

So tied between words

Where my words are unable

To say anything, by writing

A few words my pen can feel peace.

SANJAY NAIK

COMPILER

ANAMIKA

Anamika is an art preceptor by profession.

She belongs to Brass city Moradabad, Uttar Pradesh.

She loves to articulate her thoughts and views in a poetic manner.

It gives her peace and satisfaction. She has participated in 125+ anthologies before this.

Here are some of the thoughts and views expressed by Anamika,

hope you all will like it…..

Follow her on Insta @Anamika.Writes

SHADOW LOVE

In harsh rays of

Sadness and sorrows,

I was wandering in

Search of love in meadows,

Being disheartened as

I started losing heart,

You entered in my life as unknown shadow and

Became its important part…

Your true love and care nurtured,

My sadness into happiness

My snivel's into laughter's,

Your unconditional love bring us close

You are my only energy dose,

For you I am possessive as a kiddo

Can walk blindly,

BEHIND YOUR SHADOW

ANAMIKA

1.   Antara Choudhary

अंतरा चौधरी, नागपुर महाराष्ट्र की निवासी हैं । वह पिछले कुछ सालों से लिख रही हैं। उन्हें लिखने का शौक हैं । वह कहती हैं की जज़्बातों को लिखकर ज़ाहिर करने से दिल को सुकून मिलता हैं और लिखकर दिल की बात ज़ाहिर करना भी एक कला हैं।
उन्हें पढ़ना और लिखना दोनों पसंद हैं ।
वो खुद को खुशनसीब मानती हैं की वह बहुत ही सरल भाषा में लिखती हैं
ताकि सब पढ़ सकें।
संपर्क करने हेतु -
इंस्टाग्राम - antarachoudhury.15

तुझे पाकर मेरा इश्क़ मुकम्मल हुआ...

तेरी ओर मैं खींची चली जाऊं,
लाख कोशिशे करूँ रोकने की खुदको,
बस तेरी बातों में हर बार आ जाऊं,

तेरे नशीली आँखों में
मैं यूँ खो जाऊं,
रूठने की वजह भी मैं भूल जाऊं,

ख्वाबों में तेरे यूँ खो जाऊं,
तेरे बिना मैं एक पल भी जीना पाऊं,

तेरी एक मुस्कुराहट देखकर,
अपने सारे ग़मों को भूल जाऊं,

इश्क़ के दरिये में यूँ खोना है,
मुझे ये ज़िन्दगी बस तेरे संग ही बितानी है ,
तू ही तो है मेरा संसार सारा,
तुझे पाकर मेरा इश्क़ मुकम्मल हुआ ।।

----अंतरा चौधरी

2. Shivam Maurya

इनका नाम :~ शिवम् मौर्या
यह गोरखपुर उत्तर प्रदेश से हैं।
ये दिल से एक लेखक और गायन के बारे में भावुक।
वह अपने पाठकों के बीच प्यार और सकारात्मकता
फैलाना चाहता है और अपने जादुई शब्दों से अपने पाठकों
के दिलों पर मरहम लगाना चाहता है।
शिवम सबसे ज्यादा शांतमय है
उनका मानना है कि उनके शब्दों की शक्ति, कई पाठकों
के घावों को ठीक कर देगी।

"जिंदगी"

जिंदगी को समझने लगा हूँ ।।

ख़्वाब से अब ज़रा जगने लगा हूँ
जिंदगी को बेहतर समझने लगा हूँ ।

उड़ता था शायद कभी ऊँचा हवा में ,
जमीं पर अब पैदल चलने लगा हूँ ।

लफ़्ज़ों की हमे ज़रूरत नहीं है ,
चेहरों को जब से पढ़ने लगा हूँ ।

थक जाता हूँ अक्सर इन शोर से ,
ख़ामोशियों से बातें करने लगता हूँ ।

दुनियाँ की बदलती तस्वीर देख कर ,
शायद मैं भी कुछ कुछ बदलने लगा हूँ ।

नफ़रत के ज़हर को मिटाना ही होगा ,
इरादा यह मज़बूत करने लगा हूँ ।

परवाह नहीं कोई साथ आए मेरे ,
मैं अकेले ही आगे बढ़ने लगा हूँ ।

3. Har Deepansh Bahadur Sinha

हर दीपाँश बहादुर सिन्हा लखनऊ, उत्तर प्रदेश से संबंध
रखते है।
इन्होंने नैशनल पोस्ट ग्रेजुएट कॉलेज से भूगोल में स्नाकोत्तर
की शिक्षा गृहण की है।
गाने सुनना, पकवान बनाना , गाड़ी चलाना इनकी रुचियाँ
है।
लिखना , तस्वीरे लेना , सौरमंडल को समझना और घूमने
के प्रति इनका गहरा लगाव है।

सिलसिला किस्मत का

यदि किस्मत चलना चाहे साथ
तो बेशक आगे बढ़ाना अपना हाथ ,
किस्मत की रेखा होती महत्वपूर्ण
ज़िंदगी में आनंद होता संपूर्ण ।

यदि उसने चुना है तुम्हे हमसफर
तो बेशक सम्भालेगी वह तुम्हारी डगर ,
किस्मत के लिए भी करो प्रयास
तब जाकर होगा खुशी का एहसास ।

अच्छे अच्छों को नहीं मिलता प्यार
बस ज़िंदगी गुज़र जाती करते इंतजार ,
तो किसी की ना रुकती तकरार
उजड़ जाता बसा बसाया संसार ।

जिसके लिए अच्छी उसके लिए सौभाग्य
जिसके लिए बुरी उसके लिए दुर्भाग्य ,
जैसे मनुष्य की है दिखावटी पोशाक
किस्मत के भी कर दिए दो भाग ।

सदैव खुली रखना उसके लिए अपनी बाँहें
कभी मत करना उससे अलग अपनी राहें ,
यदि ना प्राप्त हुआ परम सुख
बेशक बदलेगा हवा का रुख ।

4. Sonali Meher

यह सोनाली मेहेर है।
यह ओडिशा से है। यह BAMS की द्वितीय वर्ष की छात्रा है।
यह पेशे से एक डाक्टर हैं और शौक से एक अच्छी
लेखिका हैं ।
इन्हें लिखना बहुत पसंद है। इन्होंने अलग अलग बुक के
लिए लिखा है।
Instagram id:-Sonalimeher124

जिंदगी

ज़िंदगी को मना लीजिए
जो हो रहा है होने दीजिए
ज़िन्दगी में सब अच्छा ही होता हैं ।
पर दिल मानता ही नहीं
जितना खुशी होने से भी
और खुशियाँ चाहता है ।
इन हँसी, खुशी,गम,आँसू में
जीना ही ज़िंदगी कहलाता है ।

5. Kalamkaar

इनका नाम कलमकार है ये उत्तराखंड के रहने वाले है ,
मगर मेरठ में रह रहे हैं ! इनको लिखना और पढ़ना पसंद
है! इन्होने 870+ अन्थोलॉजी में सेह लेखक के रूप में काम
किया है और 750+ सम्मान पत्र जीते है! इनको लिखना
और पढ़ना पसंद है!इनकी रूचि लिखने में है!इनको कर्म
पर विश्वास है फल से ज्यादा! इन्होने 20+पुस्तक में भाग
लिया है सह लेखक के रूप में जो रिकॉर्ड के लिए गयी है!

समय बदलते ही लोग भी बदल जाते है!

काम जब तुमसे पड़ता है उनका सगे तुम्हारे बन जाते है!
तुम्हारा काम पड़ जाये तो किनारा वो तुमसे कर जाते है!
रिश्ते जो बनाये भुला उनको देते है!
समय बदलते ही लोग भी बदल जाते है!
छोड़कर तुम्हें वो आगे बड़ जाते है!
खुदको ना जाने क्या समझ वो जाते है!
कामयाबी दूसरों की देख नहीं सकते है!
समय बदलते ही लोग भी बदल जाते है!
दिल तुम्हारा हर बार दुखाते है!
भावनाओं को ठेस वो पहुँचाते है!
अहंकार अपने अंदर भरते है!
समय बदलते ही लोग भी बदल जाते है!
आगे बढ़ते है खुद मदद तुम्हारी नहीं करते है!
जो किया तुम्हारे लिये किसी ने वो भूल जाते है!
बहाने वो तुम्हारे काम जिस्से टल जाये वो बनाते है
समय बदलते ही लोग भी बदल जाते है!

©kalamkaar

6. Ankur Mishra

बातें अपनी दिल की इस कदर किया करते हैं,
जज़बात को बयां कोरे पन्ने मे किया करते हैं।
ये हैं अंकुर मिश्रा जो वर्तमान मे देवास मध्यप्रदेश मे
कार्यरत एक उभरते हुए लेखक हैं जो कि जिंदगी और
नौकरी का संतुलन बनाये रखते हुए अपने लेखन के शौक
को जिंदा रखे हुए हैं। इनकी रचनाये पच्चीस से ज्यादा ई-
बुक/किताबो मे प्रकाशित हो चुकी या होने वाली हैं। भविष्य
मे ये अपनी सभी रचनाओ को खुद की पुस्तक मे संजोने
का ख्वाब रखते हैं। इंस्टाग्राम मे आप इनसे अपने विचार
ankdip2801 मे साझा कर सकते हैं ।

शाम

सुबह उठ कर दिन भर भागते,
सोते कम ज्यादा है जागते,
इनमे से कई मौके है काम के,
रह के देखे बिना तामझाम के,
निपटा दफ्तर के सारे काम,
होते रास्ते लंबे और सड़कें जाम,
आकर मिलती तुम दामन थाम,
और पुकारती फिर मेरा नाम,
रूह को मिल जाता आराम,
जन्नत हो जाती ये हसीं शाम,
भूलभुलैया में खोजते है अकसर,
चाबी जैसे सवालों के ताले में ,
वैसे खोजें अस्तित्व का अक्स,
शाम के सुरमई उजालों में ।

7. Prakash Turiya (Raghuwanshi)

प्रकाश तुरिया, मध्य प्रदेश के बैतूल जिले की कोल् नगरी
पाथाखेड़ा के रहने वाले हैं।
इनकी उच्च शिक्षा मास्टर इन फार्मेसी हैं।
अपने जीवन के कई पड़ाव के बाद इन्होंने सफलताओ का
मुकाम हासिल किया है।
आज ये एक international जर्नल में कार्यरत हैं।

जाने क्यूँ इबादतों का असर हुआ बेअसर।।।।

अब नही किसी को किसी की खबर।
अब लगता है सबको सबसे डर।
जाने क्यूँ इबादतों का असर हुआ बेअसर।

यूँ तो लगता है, दिल बहुत दुःखता है।
अपनी ही सिसकियों से, अब डर बहुत लगता है।
अरमानो को अधूरा कर।
जाने क्यूँ इबादतों का असर हुआ बेअसर।

कब तक संभालेंगे अपने आप को।
कब तक झेलेंगे इस अभिशाप को।
ख्वाहिशों को पूरा कर।
जाने क्यूँ इबादतों का असर हुआ बेअसर।

8. Prakhar Raghuwanshi

Prakhar Raghuwanshi from Betul city of Madhya
Pradesh. He is 15 years old, currently studying in
class 12th.
He have been involved in the field of writing
specially poetry,
since last one year.

अगर....

अगर अँधेरा न होता,
तो उजाला भी किस प्रकाश का होता।
अगर दुःख न होता,
तो सुख भी किसके साथ का होता।
अगर बुराई न होती,
तो अच्छाई भी किस बात की होती।
अगर रात न होती,
तो सुबह भी किस शुरुआत की होती।

9. Priyanshu Kumar Pandey

प्रियांशु पांडे, उम्र 16 वर्ष अमरावती महाराष्ट्र के रहने वाले है।ये आदरणीय अभिराज पांडे और संगीता पांडे के पुत्र है।इनका जन्म गया बिहार में हुआ था किंतु इन्होंने सिर्फ 9 महीने की उम्र में अमरावती महाराष्ट्र की तरफ अपने कदम बढ़ा लिए।जिंदगी ने बड़ी छोटी उम्र में इनसे बहोत कुछ छीन लिया। पेशे से एक विद्यार्थी और लिखने का शौख रखते है। ये इससे पहले 15 से अधिक किताबो के लिए कविताएं लिख चुके है। इनका मानना कुछ इस प्रकार है कि कविता चरित्र को दर्शाती है।ये सोचते है कि कमियाब होने के लिए उम्र मायने नहीं रखती। इन्हे लगता है हुनर को अवसर की तलाश होती है। कलम के सहारे दुनिया को शब्दों में पिरो कर कागज पर उतारने का जज़्बा रखते है तथा ख्वाब को हकीकत नहीं बल्कि हक़ीक़त को खूबसूरती से अपनाना चाहते है।
आस पास होती अच्छाई बुराई को कलम के जरिए कागज पर व्यक्त करना चाहते है।।
Insta I'd -Priyanshu pandey 2184

ज़ख्म - ए - इश्क

छोड़ सबसे बात करना
अब खामोश रहना
अच्छा लगने लगा है
धोखे का मरहम लगा गई वो
अब चोट खाना ही
अच्छा लगने लगा है
जब छोड़ गई मुझको यूँ
अब तनहाई में गुनगुनाना
अच्छा लगने लगा है
शब्द कहने कि तो वजह ही चली गई
तो खामोशी का बहाना ही
अच्छा लगने लगा
आज जब अकेला हो गया हूँ
नहीं कोई साथ देने वाला
तो कोने में यूँ बैठ
बिना कुछ कहे यूँ मुस्कुराना
अच्छा लगने लगा है
अच्छा लगने लगा है

10. Shivang Sharma

शिवांग शर्मा आज के युग के नए शायर हैं। शायर साहब वाराणसी के निकट स्थित मऊ जिले से आते हैं। इन्होंने कई पुस्तकों में सह - लेखक और संकलक के रूप में काम किया हैं। शायर साहब वर्तमान समय में राष्ट्रीय प्रौद्योगिकी संस्थान पटना से इंजीनियरिंग कर रहे हैं।
इनके लिखने का सिलसिला क्यूँ शुरू हुआ ये आपको नीचे के लेख में दिखेगा -
" मिलता नहीं मुझे कोई
अकेला रहता हूँ मैं ,
लेता हूँ सहारा कलम का
पन्नों पे चीख देता हूँ मैं। "

Insta I'd -
@__dil_e_alfaaz__

क्या बनाया

मेमार तुने ये क्या बनाया
न सुख हैं यहाँ...
ना ही किसी बुजुर्ग का साया,

कैद है घरों में
ऐसे की जानों,

घर, घर न हो
घर हो एक कैद खाना।

10. Poetry Khakholia

नमस्कार, ये है पोइट्री खाखोलिया
गुवाहाटी असम से, बीयालिस वर्ष, कॉन्वेंट एजुकेटेड ,
शादीशुदा दो बच्चे है।
इन्होंने एमकॉम,
म.इड, एलएलबी किया है पर लिखना
इनकी रुचि रही है स्कूल से ही और अब इसी क्षेत्र में एक
मुकाम अर्जित करना चाहती।
इन्होंने चालीस से ज्यादा अंथोलॉजी में अपनी लेखनी से
नवाजा है और कहानी किताब भी लिख रही है जो जल्द ही
आने वाली। लिखना सिर्फ काम नहीं बल्कि जुनून है इनके
लिए जो ये हर पल जीती।
आशा है आप सभी को इनकी रचना पसंद आए।

अब तो छाया भी साथ नहीं

ये शाम भी मेरी तनहाई जैसी है
उदास और अकेली ।
ढलते सूरज के साथ मैं भी ढलने लगी हूं
सूखे साख की भांति अब मुरझा रही हूं ।
तेरे आने की अब कोई ओट नहीं
कोई अब आरजू भी नहीं ।
अब किसी से कोई गीले शिकवे भी नहीं
शिकायतों की लंबी फैरिस्ट भी नहीं ।
अब तो साया भी साथ नहीं
बस अब आदत सी हो गई
कोई शुभा कोई मलाल नहीं ।
मैं तो इस शाम से भी रिश्ता बना चुकी
अब किसी रिश्ते की जरूरत नहीं।

By: पोइट्री खाखोलिया

12. ANKITA NAHAR

#AKII#@@@ अंकिता नाहर मूल रूप से अजमेर, राजस्थान की रहने वाली हैं। ये लिखने के लिए हमेशा उत्साहित रहती है साथ ही हमेशा शब्दों से सुकून सा पाती हैं। ये अपने विचारों और जो भी इन्होंने अपनी जिंदगी से सीखा है, अनुभव लिया है उसे अपनी रचनाओं में लिख देती हैं। इससे इनकी रचनाएँ बहुत ही ज्यादा भावुक भावों वाली और प्रभावशाली बन जाती हैं। जो कि पढ़ने वालों को बहुत आकर्षित करती है। वह इस माध्यम को और आगे तक ले जाना चाहती हैं। आप इनकी रचनाओं को इंस्टाग्राम @naharankita1 पर पढ़ सकते हैं।

ज़िन्दगी की किताब मैं कुछ पन्ने लिखे जा चुके हैं,
और कुछ पन्ने लिखना बाकी हैं।

पर जितने भी पन्ने अभी तक लिखे जा चुके हैं ,
उनमें सबसे खूबसूरत पन्नों में से एक वो भी हैं।

जिसे मैंने अपनी ज़िन्दगी के साथ साथ ,
अपनी डायरी में भी लिखा हैं।

और वो मात्र डायरी नहीं है,
बहुत खास हैं मेरे लिए।

वैसे तो मैं अपनी डायरी में,
हर एक बात लिखती हूं।

जो बात में किसी से ना कहना चाहूं,
उन सब बातों को मैं डायरी में लिख आऊ।

जब कोई नहीं होता पास मेरे
उस समय तुम साथ होती हो मेरे।

तुम जीवन का एक बड़ा हिस्सा हो मेरा,
या यूं कहूं प्रतिबिंब हो तुम मेरा।

©AKII#@@@

13. Ravishanker Nishad (ARVI)

यह रविशंकर निषाद है ।

ये   शाखा :- तमनार, जिला :- रायगढ़ (छत्तीसगढ़) के निवासी हैं ।

इनका जन्म 19 जून 2000 में हुआ था ।

यह अभी इंजीनियरिंग कॉलेज में पढ़ाई कर रहे है ।

इनकी रुचि कविताएं लिखना है और यह किताबों के शौकीन भी है ।।

तजुर्बा है एक सीख है, चोरी से बेहतर भीख है ।
मेहनत करो खूब से बहुत खूब तलाश करो
दरिया मिल जाय अगर तो समुंदर की तलाश करो
थक कर हारना नहीं है कभी
मन के मारे रहना नहीं है कभी ।।
हौसलों की उम्मीदें बढाओ आगे बढ़ो
फिर पीछे मुड़कर देखना नहीं है ।।
हर शख्स गहरी राज लिए फिरता है
मतलब का कुछ काम हो तभी मिलता है ।।
गैर ही अच्छे इन मामलातों में
जाने बिना ही मदद किया करते हैं ।।
दोस्ती का फ़र्ज़ वो
हक से अदा किया करते हैं ।।
जनलो दुनिया की हकीकत है फसाना है
हाथों में नोट हो तभी जमाना है ।।

Ravishanker Nishad (ARVI)

14. Bhawna Mehta

She is presently pursuing B.Ed from Guru
Jambheshwar University,Hisar.

She likes to pen down her thoughts.

She has written two Blogs and won Blog
Competition also.

उम्मीद ना करो किसी से,
हौंसला खुद करो,
विश्वास खुद पर रखो,
मन में ठान कर तुम आगे बढ़ो,
मंजिल ज़रूर मिलेगी,
नियत अगर साफ़ होगी,
तो कामयाबी अवश्य मिलेगी,
एक बार हार कर,
रुक मत जाना,
वहीं से तुम दोबारा शुरू करना।

15. Anjali Samundre

Anjali!! From Jabalpur MP. She is19.
She is a commerce student.
She started writing since last 5 years.

अपना

मुझे पतझड़ के मौसम में,
सावन सा प्यार करने वाला चाहिए।
मुझे इस समझदार सी दुनिया में,
नासमझ से प्यार करने वाला चाहिए।
मुझे गैरो से इस जहान में,
अपना बनाने वाला चाहिए।
मुझे मतलबी लोगो के बीच,
बेमतलब सा प्यार करने वाला चाहिए।
मुझे राम की इस पावन भूमि में,
श्री कृष्ण सा प्यार करने वाला चाहिए।
मुझे रॉयल एनफील्ड चलाने के ज़माने में,
स्प्लेंडर चलाने वाला चाहिए।
मुझे प्यार जताने से ज्यादा,
प्यार निभाने वाला चाहिए।
मुझे सात समंदर पार ले जाने वाला नही,
केदारनाथ के दर्शन कराने वाला चाहिए।
मुझे गैरो के इस जहान में,
अपना बनाने वाला चाहिए।।

#अंजली

16.Yogesh Gurjar Chinu

इनका नाम योगेश गुर्जर है और निकनेम चीनू है,
यह उत्तरप्रदेश के गौतम बुद्ध नगर जिले से है।

इन्हें थॉट्स लिखना और पढ़ना बहुत पसंद है,
पोएट्री और कोट्स 1300 से ज्यादा लिख चुकी है।

450 Anthology में Co-author के रूप में लिख चुकी है।
इनकी पहली सोलो बुक जिसका नाम (सच्ची बातें "चीनू")
है।

ख्वाबों का अफ़साना

मिल जाये कोई बहाना,
मिल जाये कोई ठिकाना,

कि थोडा सा जी लूं मै भी,
मिल जाये कोई वजह जीने की,

मिल जाये कोई तराना,
मिल जाये कोई अफ़साना,

चलो वादा नही हो चाहे कोई
मिल जाये कोई यादों का सफीना,

मिल जाये कोई दीवाना,
मिल जाये कोई अवाना,

उम्र गुजर जाये फिर सारी
बस हो जाये इक छोटा सा बहाना,

जिन्दगी गुजर जाये बे रोक टोक
हो इक छोटा सा आशियाना....!!

17.Kajal Bhargav

काजल भार्गव यह लखनऊ से है इन्हे लिखना , पढ़ना ,
घूमना पसंद है यह भविष्य में लेखक और अध्यापक बनना
चाहती है इनका सपना अनाथ आश्रम बनाने का है।
हर उड़ान ऊंची उड़ जाऊ ये जरूरी नहीं
बस हर उड़ान खुलकर उड़ पाऊं ये जरूरी है।

उड़ान....

उड़ने के लिए पंख नही हौंसला चाहिए
उम्मीदों का एक जहां और ऊंची उड़ान हो
टूट कर बिखरे तो अपनो की गोद चाहिए
जब हम उड़े तो न उसमे कोई रोक हो।
पंछी बन कर उड़ने के लिए साथ चाहिए
धरती या आसमा पर भी अपना ही जोर हो
सपनो को जोड़ने के लिए डोर चाहिए
जिस राह पर चले हम न उसमे कोई मोड़ हो
मुझे जो थाम सके ऐसा कोई साथ चाहिए
लड़के लड़की में उड़ान को लेके न कोई भेद हो ।

18.   AAYUSHI KHEDIA

Co-author Aayushi Khedia is a student from Purulia, West Bengal. She can't express much and that is the reason why she started writing.
She believes sometimes words speak. Through her shayaris, she tries to express her feelings.
She is not a writer by profession but writing is her passion. She wrote her first shayari when she was 9 yrs old. She still remembers that day. Firstly she gives the credit to her mom. Her mother is an exceptional writer but is not famed by others.
She thanks 'Your Quote' too that gave her a platform to flourish her writings. She wants to thank her father who always supported her.
She wish that he could see this and is determined to make him proud one day. She always try to write not for fame but for the love of her readers.

तुझे पाकर जिंदगी का मतलब है समझ आया ,
तेरा होकर मैंने सब कुछ हैं पाया ।
मेरी जिंदगी में एक सुनहरा सा उपहार हो तुम ,
तेरे ही प्यार में हो गई हूं गुम।
प्यार सा लगता है हर अहसास ,
तेरे साथ लगता है बहुत खास ।
नहीं मिला कोई आजतक तेरे जैसे ,
जो दिल से न हुआ हो वो प्यार ही कैसा ♡ ♡

ENGLISH

She is Lipsa Dabhi.
She is an Author and also a good Co-Author.
She is eighteen years old. She is a student of
computer engineering.
She is an extraordinary person. She is always a good
leader.
Her mam Mrunal Prajapati is her inspiration person
and also her motivator, her friend Chetna Raval also
supported her and her mom Manisha ben and her
father Nilesh Bhai also supported her for any type of
her creativity.
She also wrote poems, short stories, and shayaris.
Her writing skills are almost very well and her
creative collections are always best.

"Father is shadow"

Father is shadow of my life,
Father is unique personality for me,
Father is best supporter ever,
Father is a special and perfect part of life.

Father is best person of life,
Father is extraordinary person,
Father is strength of my life,
Father is best friend forever.

Father is caring and sharing partner,
Father is always best guidelines forever,
Father is super hero of my life,
Father is everything of my life.

20.   Mohammed Niyaz

Mohammed Niyaz hails from Mumbai - The City of
Dreams.
He often loves to write poetries and short music
Video stories for his own YouTube channel.
Apart from this Mohammed is currently working on
his upcoming anthologies,
As well writing poetries since 2013.
You can find him on Facebook/Mohammed Niyaz as
well on instagram @niyazsks.

Stage of Troubles

Teeth falling from old to permanent.
Fear of losing all is the biggest incident.

From one to ten table exists in those minds.
Sickness of memory loss till they find.

Hopes that live with in alive.
For a moment when they are live.

Laughter is the best medicine.
Sadness behind tears of acne.

Pimples that never say goodbye.
Today or tomorrow face without shy.

Curiosity of career they think about.
Never gonna be ready to thought.

Missions of success is the dream.
Failures are co-members of the team.

Life is all about experiencing "stage of troubles".
At every single moment they might be getting
doubles.

21. Harshita Verma

Co-author Harshita Verma is a writer from Lucknow.
She has completed her graduation in commerce
stream.
She has been writing poetry for the last few years as
her passion.
She wants to be a novelist in future.

God

Believe in God He will fulfil your dreams
Talk to him He will take all your fears
He will give you the hope to rise
Believing Him will lead you to believe in the miracles
that He does.

Have faith in God that He is there
Ready to support against the flare
He will be present by your side everytime
Having faith in him will make you complete
monstrous tasks in time.

Love God like a child loves his father
Do not question His actions
As he does what is best for you
Love Him without any conditions He will take away
all your troubles.

22. Priya Singh

Priya Singh is born & brought up in Dewas,
MadhyaPradesh.
She's a Proud daughter of her Father B.N.Singh
(T.I.).She's completed Masters of Computer
Science.She is a Former Educationist,
Communication Trainer & Avid Reader.
She's the Co-Author of the Anthologies:-
"It's all about two phase : love & hate" ,"Words From
Heart", "Fierce, Fearless N Flawed" & "In the way of
borehole", "Unseen Blessings & "Sublime Love",
"Mere Papa".
All are available in Amazon.
Till today, She's worked in 200+ Anthologies as a
Co-Author & compiling 3.
Her writing keeps her at ease.
She mostly write quotes on thoughts.
She loves inspiring young minds.
Instagram id- instant__thoughts_

/Midnight - Musings//

You aren't mine but sometimes

You're all I want as musings,

Sometimes thrilling & chilling

Aghast while being with you,

Everything seems so viewed

& lovable so true, isn't it weird

Nothing seems so glue until

You come & make it hue.

Some journeys meant to still,

They never take us anywhere,

But give us most valuable lessons

Of life, some journeys are never journeys though.

I don't know if I'll be brave enough to let go,

Let go, who??

My fears, worries, anxieties,

That never let me be "Me"

Always pushed me to be

Something that I never ever

Supposed to be.

23.   Dhritishree Rani Baruah

Hey, Beautiful Souls, This is Dhritishree,
Just a normal traveller in the journey of life,
Discovering herself day by day.
I'm a school going girl from Assam, loads of love.

Waves of love!

Infinite feelings in a breathe,
Millions of dreams in an eye blink.

Vibrations of pride going through my body,
And Aerosols of love hugging me close.

Rainbows of love in the reddish sky,
And cosmos of pleasure in my heart.

The rays of day star makes me feel confident,
The rise of Venus before sunrise makes me beautiful.

Beach foam gives me goosebumps of fear,
But the night stars makes me more vibrant.

The creamy clouds are going to be thunder soon..

I'm just a droplet of rain,
Floating with the waves of love!

24.Shaswat Sourav Sahoo (Shassy)

Shaswat Sourav Sahoo, is an eighteen-something
adventurer who grew up traversing the wonders
through the pages of metaphors. He fell in love with
books and never reverted. Today he is pursuing his
studies and living a clichéd life at NISER as an
Integrated M.Sc. Research scholar. He has been
recently awarded with the Global Achiever's Award.
When he is not resounded by words you can spot him
fancying and pampering the dogs. He is a jovial kind
of person revamping his past grief events into allured
moments. He loves voicing his emotions and get it
penned down. Another feather to his cap is his intense
intimacy with taking shots.
Nevertheless, he is also impassioned for painting,
playing indoors, origami. He is looking forward his
life being a polymath and pour on whatever he
possesses within and wishes never to quell it.

Behind my Shadow

The omniscient is there,
Watching and propagating so far,
The world under his arms,
Near to heart, yet so far.

Objective is one, Goal is two,
Responsibility is three and many more to do.
Is what folks take birth for,
With some qualities that fits in their shoe.

Booked was my Destiny,
To be bright and shine right,
To handle stuffs and be tight,
With all the courage and my might.

I lost my near ones,
Dear and adorable ones,
But the right ones
Always stay as the Forever ones

© Shaswat Sourav Saho

25. Prachi Gupta

Prachi Gupta is a Passionate writer who loves to create her imaginary arts in a random canvas. She is pursuing her studies in BBA and lives in Allahabad known as The pure city of Sangam.

She loves to sing and watching movies in her free time. She is a shy and a open-minded girl at the same time
For more information can follow her and contact:-
Prachiguptt0210@gmail.com

@prachigupta3435
@prachi_gupta_210

MORE POWER TO YOU

If you feel Low
I send you power

If you feel Weak
I send you Strength

If you feel Bad
I send you some good moments

If you feel Alone
I send you company to rejoin

If you feel Distracted
I send you some meditation tips

If you feel disturbed
I send you some happiness

If you feel depressed
I send you some energy to feel Joy

26.   Sakshi jarandikar

Since childhood she loves writing immensely, after a
graduation she converted her passion into profession
,she is now based in pune.Her first an e book was on
romance , second book (debut book of paperback)will
be soon publishing on hope and motivation.Apart
from that she likes to paint and act it out. She recently
started her show called "dil ki baatein " on
Spotify app.
She shares special bond with her audience.

Cause all I need you.

It is good day ,

With a smile ,

A hot coffee ,

And warm weather ,

I dreamt about you ,

I felt about some or few ,

cause all I need you !

Now,

You're in my head ,

Everybody's ain't game ,

All I have just to say ,

All I want give a way ,

Maybe you have just of it,

Maybe you have all of it,

cause all I need you .

The night is blooming with colours ,

And the ocean reaches to the   shores,

Star is just shining ,

That what's your eyes do ,

Maybe I'm wrong ,

Maybe I'm right,

Maybe I have all of it, Cause I left in few of you !

Cause all I need you !

27.   S.Suganthi

Suganthi has been writing for over two years.

She provides philosophical writings.

Her educational background in English literature has

given her

a broad base for writings.

Her books are available in

Amazon Kindle named Heartily Sayings and

Healing journey-11

Karma

Pain is gone, I feel happy
And everything is over.
But whenever I see the scars,
It reminds me of the past.
Scars motivate me to grow.
The pain in me can be reduced.
But I still remember the lesson.
Karma is real.
So l believe everything will
Be alright one day.

28.   Madhumitha / madhu

A conscious dreamer letting her thoughts out through
pen and paper

True

In this generation,

Trusting someone is like

Preparing poison by yourself

And drinking it at the end.

Some words are like lamp,

Enters into heart,

Lighten up our soul.

Some words are like gloom,

Enters into brain,

Darkens our soul.

Go to settings of your life,

Deactivate your past,

Activate your optimism,

And Reboot your life!!

29. Sonal Prajapati

I am Sonal Prajapati living in Delhi.

Electrical Engineer by profession and writer by

passion.

I had been part of online writing contest and books

like the cage of soul, jeevansathi, the inked solace,

classy lassie, hope- a positive vibes, colleen warriors,

soliloquy, twinkling versus, Nzare unke, love is

everything, Incarnation and hope- faith & trust, love-a

journal, friendship a book, kuch lamhe yaadon ke ,

satrangi barsaat , ishq ke raste, lines from the heart,

Tu jo mere sath hai

My life partner

In a world of full confusion

You are the one which is my compulsion

I carry all my desire

Because I want to be your fire

Having your hug in a day

It is like a shower in month of may

You carry my stuff all the time

Your every words matches words of mine

Your heart pumps thinking about me

Only this thing I can see, see, see

You are a true blessing to my life

I really really want to be your wife.

30. Akkshaya prasanna

Contagious smile, anxious heart, conscious mind,
Gracious she

Better being alone

Bitter feeling alone

She love being alone

Not feeling alone

My shadow provoked me to think

About the feelings that lift me

That's being alone

But feeling alone is quite different

It pulls me down

Depress me down

Will scratch my head

To think about haters

Its feel like on heaters

I know it's warm

But it harm

I am not happy

Loneliness is crappy

Just wrap it

Throw it

See you

Feel you

Love you

31.Ankita Mishra

She is Ankita Mishra from Cuttack, Odisha.
She is a student pursuing her graduation in bachelor's
of commerce.
Writing was never her passion nor her hobby. All she
loved was singing, crafting and playing badminton.
Then when she used to stay alone her fears and
feelings started haunting her and there was when she
started writing her feelings no matter happy or sad
into words. She is just hoping to take forward her
writing and taking this habit as her passion.
Your imperfections makes you perfect,
Your flaws makes you flawless.

MAGIC IN YOUR SMILE

And in her smile he see something
more beautiful than the moon.
Something that takes away,
all of his gloom.
Whenever she smiles,
it takes away his breath !
She holds the power of magic
for him to get mesmerised.
She don't need a foundation,
nor does she need a blush !
The beauty her smile holds,
leaves in him with a rush.
Though the moon has scars,
yet it shines so bright.
Her smile holds the purity,
that's brighter than the moonlight.

32.Ananya P Mishra

She is a girl with lot of patience and as calm as sea. Her name is Ananya P Mishra from Bhubaneswar, Odisha. She is pursuing her graduation in English Honors. Bedsides that she is an Interior designer, Graphic designer. One of the brand Ambassador of PWI. Participated in more than 100 anthologies.

She has been an active participant in literary arts, competitions. Believes in karma. Bookaholic.Want to set an example for this era that inspires others and me as well. Love dancing, writing, exploring new things.

Self-love is priority.

Always know your worth.

The Reason is you-

My days are for you

My Nights are for you

My rests are only for you

You are my today

You are my tomorrow

All my moments are for you,

there is your foot-prints on the

land of my heart.

I want to be in your breaths

I want to be in your arms

Such that no-one may make us apart.

33.   Dakshita Jaiswal

Dakshita jaiswal is a 18 year old

Management student.

She is from Gonda, Uttarpradesh.

Being a voracious reader and writer,

She has organized multiple events and itself is a poet,

storyteller, blogger and a published author.

She is the core team member of Happy hearts

organization, an event organizing house. She

inculcates high interest into the field of writing and

have performed at various platforms.

You can search her on Instagram

@invoicer_dakshita_jaiswal

Can I be my last hope?

Yesterday, My hope cried for Eight hours,
Wrecked with emotions, My Believe went dark,
Dark in the slimmer silver lining of clouds, bursting
with Pain of doubts,
Doubt that awakens me from my Dream of shroud,
Breaths couldn't reside my heart,
Eyes were frozen with Arch's,
Swelled up throat, dead mouth to erode,
Blooded limps, with a mark of Failure,
Failure that could deceive My Faith,
Could one nerve can shut their Says?
Bearing the unbearable pain,
My heartbeats were leaving my soul in vain,
Bewildered by shiva's Plan,
Drenched with Betrayal, Disrupted to trust His Idol,
My mind was clogged,
In the dim light that agogs, across my faith and my
trusts,
Challenging my esteem to build upon a thrust,
Thrust which holds the gesture to fight,
A thrust which could Enlight,
My fear would be my last shroud untill shiva's
delight,
Reckoned to hear, but enough of tears,
Love to rebel and hate to deny,
Filch destiny, Let's conquer and fly high,
Let's cease the story,
Through revenge of Glory,
Of countless cries, I pledge to fly,
Can I be my last hope?
Hope that smiles with divine eternity,
Promises to learn, live and love,
with Eccentricity,
To be my labour of love,
Hope with an oath of Desire,
An inevitable end of arousing fire.
- Dakshita jaiswal

34.Dharshini. M

She is dharshini from kovilpatti.

She is pursing masters in English.

She has huge interest in writing.she loves to share her

thought and emotion through her writing.

She has done many anthologies as co author .

She has published a book named 'vox of mine '.

Shadows

Shadows states a better knowledge
That everyone leaves when time comes
Shadow will follow us all time
But in darkness
It left us
You are the one who fight for you
You are the one stands for your wish
Believe and fight
Everything will comes
Under your feet

35.SRIJA SADHUKHAN

Srija Sadhukhan is 19 years old girl studying BSc
Biotechnology in Amity University Kolkata. Love to
write poetry and a book worm too.

FRIEDEN

My life wasn't a curse,

I traveled across the borders in search of me

But found myself in the middle of nowhere

Kept search for peace in the silence

And realized it lies in the stillness

My heart needs silence of my heart.

The inner soul scream and wanted to grasp me,

But the only thing I really want is peace.

Though searching for peace everywhere

Thousand thoughts crossed my mind

Went to a secluded place and isolate myself

To find peace in my hearts corner

But I forgot to looked within

And I found peace in myself.

36.Mansi Solanki

Mansi Solanki from Navsari, Gujarat.
She is currently pursing diploma civil engineering
from Uka Tarsadia university.
She have started writing a month ago and she loves to
write poems, shayari, quotes, oneliner.
She is CoAuthor of 40+ anthologies and thank you
for giving her chance for this anthology.

You were like my shadow

I can see you during sunshine

Maybe I loved a little insane,

But at least I had the courage to lose myself in you.

I am proud the way

I loved you and truly wanted

As my shadow in all my ups and downs.

I lost myself in you

To only become your shadow in your sorrows and

happiness

To protect you from every disaster.

37.Anusha Sathia

Anusha is a writer and a poet hailing from India.
She is currently in high school. She has been writing
since quite a few years and that has been her passion.
She uses her positive attitude and tireless energy to
encourage others to work hard and succeed and she
writes because she enjoys expressing herself. For
more of her work, please check out her Instagram
handle: @_thelittletherapist

Between D(us)k

As the day draws to a close
And the mundane events seize
I'm reminded of you once again
And I'm put at ease

The fading sunlight casts a glow
On your pictures in my room
I feel your strong presence around me
Down to the smell of your faint perfume

In the distance the church bells ring
The same place we said "I do"
But death couldn't do us apart
Because I'm still far from over you

The others are oblivious
They tell me you're gone
They tell me I'm a lovesick fool
They tell me to move on

To them and their advice
I choose to pay no heed
How can I move on
When a part of me lies buried.

38.   Naveen Bhardwaj

Myself Naveen bhardwaj a programmer by profession
a lover of poetry maker and like reading books and
audiobooks and he has telegram channel

@TheNBbook
insta I'd na.vin7832

Loneliness

Loneliness hurts most of the time than death;
Most of the worry is caused by our own thought;
This is not because we didn't prevail in society;
We lost contact with our loved ones or anything;
It's fear of losing something that makes them into
deep thinking;
Loneliness hurts the most then broken heart;
For loneliness being busy and not evolving in social
gathering is a common to some people;
We want to hang on our self past ;
Even it is broken because we feels that it is easier and
save;
Be productive and faithful in this deadly situation;
Awaken yourself and look out for people who are
struggling to find their own light ;

39.   Rozy Paul

Her name is Rozy Paul.
She belongs to the tea-estate called Dibrugarh,Assam
.She has done M.A.in journalism.
Her hobbies are reading,gardening and cooking.
She likes travelling a lot.

At Night:

We can see our shadow at dark night where there is dim light and that shadow going behind us and we can heard the sound of fire flies.But our inner shadow always with us.In outside behind the shadow we can't see but inside we can look at ourselves and can do helpful activities.To think our inner self behind that shadow.Outside shadow sometimes leave us when there is bright light but inside shadow live with us to show us behind that we can improve on us and live better life.

40.Tahreem Afzal

Her name is Tahreem Afzal.
She has done her MS in Mathematics.
She is the author of "My Soul's Cravings".
Besides being a dream hunter, she is the girl who is
traveling on the path called 'life'. She doesn't
complain for the obstacles, she just makes sure that
her faith never gets blurry, as this is the only candle
of light which keeps her going in dark nights.

THE REGRETFUL TEARS

Through these tears,

I shed those screams

which are caged

behind my stitched lips.

This is my way

of speaking of my pain.

The pain that has its roots

in some unwanted miseries

that were set by no one else,

but by the person

whom I made my world.

This is my way

to tell u that

I had lived a lie,

believing that love gives strength

for not falling for distractions.

With him,

I lived a beautiful lie,

considering myself the queen.

With myself now,

I am living a torturous truth,

believing that I was rejected and ignored

for the the sake of some temporary glitters.

41.Surangama

Surangama is from Gujarat completed her B.Sc.
Homemaker associated with social and cultural
activities.
She love making friends travelling reading and
playing badminton.

Dilemma of my life to cope with the world
My emotions and thoughts are at war
My fragile heart wants to impress the world
But my values oppose me far
Behind your shadow my identity finds itself
Keeps it position stay in the dark
A delicate mind seek freedom for itself
Patiently wait to made it mark
My conscious mind reminds me
I am your wife
My inner self advices me that
I should strive
With wings of imagination
Want to fly on sky of creation
Longing for the satisfaction
I Want to be real myself not your reflection.

42.   Deesha Soni

Deesha Soni..a Post Graduate and M.phil adorns the
hat of a multitasker of an
educationist,artist,poet,photographer,author ,
blogger,homemaker,wife and mother...
She has 10 years experience in the field of Education
as a Professor and Coordinator.Deesha has various
publications to her credit in national and international
levels.
Deesha has various published works to her credit...
she has two books published on Amazon... named
'Just thoughts' and 'Random thoughts on
pandemic'..Kindle edition and more than 100 plus
published works on various online platforms of ..
Deesha has been twice nominated for Author of a
week award by Storymirror and has also won various
recognitions in penning stories and write-ups.. at
National and International levels...
Deesha has various published works to her credit...
she has two books published on Amazon... named
'Just thoughts' and 'Random thoughts on
pandemic'..Kindle edition has also won many prizes
in National and international levels in many write-
ups...
Deesha has also published her works in 300 plus
anthologies of multiple genres...

Ghosts....

A black shadow...a smoke...

I'm a ghost ..your senses i shall block...

I'll possess completely over your body...

And make your voice and behavior unsteady...

I'm in scariest....horrible appearence...

I'm the ghost 'Bhoot'....a past tense...

I'll freakyou out and shiver you to death...

And make your life hell... till your last breadth...

I live on dried trees and roam in graveyard....

Once under my control... getting rid of me is hard...

I'll kill your senses...and ruin your life...

To such extent that you'll harm yourself....with

knife...

I'm the dark... evil...deadly ghost...

I've got in youuuuuu.... perpetually... cumon... raise a

toast....

43.Sonali Gouda

Being the bestest version of herself,
An introverted self-hoping for a better smile every
day.
She loves to read but rarely writes.

MEANWHILE

In the wake of your shadow,

I hide myself to let go of everything.

It's the delineation I won and own

in the name of love,

wrapped me up abiding,

finding and guiding me through all the disfigured

It helps me breathe into the impeccable

and with all the strife

the mere shadow of yours

never forgets to

clear the path ahead of me

knowing that uncertainty - a definite word

might leave it's imprint of memories

from the past till the last

yet it never leaves my sight,

urges to fight

hence with every word I write

same as before and hopefully

till I move on to the further

to not lose sight of the home

that we were meant to built

someday in the near time

dealing with all the hope and healing.

The colour of pain

in the darkest prevailing nights
seem to evade of our lives
letting us be each other's peace.

44.Sheethal. G

Hey!! I am Sheethal. G from India. I express my feelings best with ink and weave beautiful free verses that are thought provoking. I draw the stories of the world to inspire and bring up positivity and encourage them to do right things. I like to spread love to the world about ways to love themselves, their body, colour and everything. Keeping my experiences aside I try my best to appreciate someone who really needs it in their life. I believe in "Whatever happens, it's for good." My aim in life is to spread happiness around.

Shadows

I turned off the light
The shadows lay down next to me
They listened when I scream
As I bury my silence and fell asleep,
I visualized a bad dream
Where the bed sheets soak up my tears
And wind kissing me goodbyes
I want to survive this bad dream,
I tore a piece of cloth
To stop it bleed,
I drank a glass of liquid
Not bothered of what it was,
Quiet when I entered to the dark room
My eyes started to bleed.

45.   Unnati Sawant

She is a budding and bubbly writer
expressing her creative mind in pen and ink.
Born in city of dreams , passionate to travel round
the world .

Unknown Shadow

Experiencing through window ;
There was a edge narrow ;
Came the peaceful air flow ;
Look behind your shadow .

Something was there to follow ;
Just opposite of rainbow ;
Filled with sorrow ;
Look behind your shadow

Sharp as arrow ;
Crossed our elbow ;
I didn't glow and know ;
But only heared slow ;
Look behind your shadow

.

46. Varshitha Madhu

This is Varshitha Madhu. She writes what she feels and spill her emotions through the hell of a piece of paper. She loves to weave poetry and being herself in a judgement world. She believes "Don't be soft hearted because this selfish world will break your heart on every step you take."

Me and my shadow

My shadow never leave my path and follows me
blindly everytime.
My shadow is my strength.
My shadow always do as like me.
It never leave me alone.
Only my shadow understand how I feel about
everyday and everything.
My shadow is my succor.
There is strong shadow where there's much light.
Shadows have more to mention.

The one who will never leave me in any situation is
my shadow.
I love my darkness too.
Shadow never lie and never leave.
Beauty of every life is created from light and shadow.
Best companion to most are shadow.
Shadows are like magic.
Somethings can only be seen within the shadows.

\

47.N. Krishnaveni

N.   Krishnaveni is an aspiring writer and a
budding poet.
One of her poems "My Beloved Damsel!" has
published in
The Literary Herald journal.
She is a co-author of many anthologies.
She won the Spectrum Budding Writer Award 2021.
Most of her poems deals with the theme of nature,
human emotions, and philosophical thoughts. Her
poetry voices out the deepest emotions and secrets
that are left unspoken and destined to be beautifully
inked. Having a creative artistic propaganda, her
writings hails from the articulate thoughts with
coherence, spontaneity and flowery language.

BLASPHEMY

Run and chase having no rest
Not your goals but the marks.
You, your thoughts should think
What we have provide you with.
No prowess should ever roar in pride
For all you be the prisoner
Of the cell I have built upon
Not a puff of smoke would evade
Without the conscious liberty of ours.
Even the course of your dark spirit
Following you in all places
Should be decided by the route
That set by the quick turn of our fingers.
Not dare to change the frame of rules any
Else nothing could saves you from
The devious trap of blasphemy.

48..Habiba Naz

Her name is Habiba Naz.
She is a student, and a girl who sees the realities
hidden behind the curtains of lies.
She craves to make her life worth living by making a
difference in this world

SELF-LOVE

Take a minute, and think about love stories you have heard in your childhood; Jack and Rose, Lara Jean and Peter Kavinsky, Heer and Ranjha etc. We all can see that each love story requires one individual to be depending on other for the pralse and for finding the reasons to feel great. Taking this out of the box, their is another relation of love that is usually ignored i.e. Self-love. While not mixing it with ego, self-love is most beautiful form of love. This is the relationship that you have with you, and that needs patience, compassion and learning. "The power of self-love is greater than any other relationship because we don't need ourselves to be smart, sexy or perfect. We just love ourselves the way we are". At some stage of life, when we are completely left alone, we feel and realize that we need to care for ourselves, and that is the stage when we start to love ourselves. When you accept yourself the way you are, when you love the imperfect existence of yourself, you actually set yourself free from a lot of boundaries which bound you to be unsatisfied with yourself. So, next time on Valentine's day, celebrate this love by giving yourself the huge treat, by promising that you will not let anyone degrade yourself, and you will always be there for your imperfect existence to dance perfectly in this chaotic world

49. ANUPAMA SAHU

Meet Anupama Sahu, a friend philosopher and guide
and an agony aunt all rolled up into one.
A voracious reader converted into a mature versatile
writer on all kinds of topics for all ages including
scripts for dramas and plays.
Being intensely emotional caring and kind hearted,
she's easily moved by sorrow and all these endearing
qualities are evident in her style of writing.

The Misunderstanding

The misunderstanding between us

Led us on different paths

In opposite directions

It was difficult to move away

I could not go away from you

I wanted you to call my name, stop me...

Clear up everything...

And renew our bond..

I feel you also wanted the same...

But none of us spoke

We both were mum and numb..

We had our ego in between

We were proud of ourselves

So we didn't stop each other

You walked away on your path and I started on my

way ...

The gap between us grew ...

It became greater and greater...

Now we are so far apart from each other..

We can never turn back and start again...

From where we left years ago..

50.NEERAJ.J

Neeraj was born on 23rd December 2000 in Chennai.
He is good at solving mathematical problems related
to life situations.
He is also a writer and writes stories, poems and also
compiled around 30 anthologies so far.
To succeed in life he always follow this
" Enjoy the goodness and the badness of the life
always".

Life with the great cost

Once a boy lived in a village named Kash and he was selling fruits in that particular village but most of them was not getting fruits which looks dry to eat and cook. Once he started to think about it and made himself what to plan next about his selling career. Then he got an idea on how to sell things that is decorated in each house. He started to cut those trees and other materials from nature which made everything destroy into pieces and he started to sell nature in terms of his live good. Then he started to become rich by selling those but unfortunately he got a memory which made him realise about what he did was totally wrong and he remembered about playing in those sweet garden and selling the fruits given by the nature as their blessings. Then he said these richness would not give back those life and he started to plant trees and save nature from where he lost the nature of his life and realizing ones wrong in selling is a good cause when richness is there still.